AF482816

EMMANUEL JOSEPH

The Power of Connection: A Woman's Guide to Building Healthy Relationships

Copyright © 2023 by Emmanuel Joseph

All rights reserved. No part of this publication may be reproduced, stored or transmitted in any form or by any means, electronic, mechanical, photocopying, recording, scanning, or otherwise without written permission from the publisher. It is illegal to copy this book, post it to a website, or distribute it by any other means without permission.

First edition

This book was professionally typeset on Reedsy.
Find out more at reedsy.com

Contents

1

Chapter 1: The Foundation of Connection

In the quiet moments of our lives, beneath the bustling surface, there exists an unspoken truth: human connection is the lifeblood of our existence. It weaves the tapestry of our experiences, shapes our identities, and influences the trajectory of our lives. In this opening chapter, we embark on a journey to understand the profound significance of connection and lay the groundwork for the transformative exploration that follows.

Defining Connection

At its core, connection is the invisible thread that links us to the world around us. It's the deep sense of belonging, the warmth of shared experiences, and the unspoken understanding that words can't fully capture. It extends beyond the casual greetings and superficial interactions of our daily lives. It's the real essence of relationships that we yearn for.

The Significance of Healthy Relationships

Healthy relationships are more than just sources of joy and companionship. They are vital for our well-being. Research has shown that people with robust social connections tend to live longer, have lower stress levels, and experience increased emotional resilience. Healthy relationships provide us with a safety net, emotional support, and the fuel to thrive in life.

Gender and Connection

Society has long placed expectations and burdens on women when it comes to building and nurturing relationships. From the stereotypes of women as the primary caregivers to the myth of women as the 'weaker sex,' these cultural constructs can affect how women perceive and approach connection. It's crucial for women to understand and navigate these influences as they strive to build authentic and healthy relationships.

Self-Reflection

As we begin this journey, I invite you to pause for a moment. Think about your own experiences with connection. What have your relationships meant to you? How have they shaped your life, your dreams, and your sense of self? Self-reflection is the first step in becoming more aware of our connection needs and building healthier, more meaningful relationships.

A Glimpse of What's to Come

In the chapters that follow, we will delve deeper into the art and science of connection. We'll explore the intricacies of self-identity, the nurturing of self-love, the embrace of vulnerability, and the development of effective communication. Together, we will unravel the secrets of trust, friendship, and romantic relationships, and we will discover how to navigate the complexities of family dynamics and maintain a balance between independence and interdependence.

"The Power of Connection" is a guide tailored for women, a compass for building and sustaining relationships that uplift and empower. So, let's embark on this journey together, for the power of connection is within your grasp, waiting to transform your life in ways you might never have imagined.

2

Chapter 2: Understanding Self-Identity

I n this chapter, we delve deep into the core of our being - self-identity. Understanding who we are at our very essence is the first step in building healthy relationships. As women, we often find ourselves influenced by societal expectations, external opinions, and the desire to meet the needs of others. However, to connect authentically with others, we must first connect with ourselves.

Exploring Self-Identity

To truly understand self-identity, we need to ask ourselves profound questions. What are your values, beliefs, and aspirations? What are your strengths, weaknesses, and unique qualities? This self-exploration is not only empowering but also essential for forming relationships that align with our true selves.

The Impact of External Influences

Throughout our lives, external factors shape our sense of self. Society, family, friends, and cultural norms can all influence our self-identity. Understanding these influences allows us to separate them from our authentic selves and make choices that are in harmony with our values and aspirations.

The Power of Authenticity

Authenticity is the cornerstone of forming meaningful connections. When we are authentic, we invite others to be themselves, fostering deeper and more genuine relationships. This chapter explores the significance of authenticity and offers practical advice on how to embrace it in your life.

The Journey of Self-Discovery

Self-identity is not static; it's a dynamic and evolving aspect of our lives. In this chapter, we discuss methods of continuous self-discovery and personal growth. We'll provide tools and exercises to help you explore your self-identity more deeply and evolve as a person, which, in turn, will enrich your relationships.

Creating a Solid Foundation

Building healthy relationships starts with a strong self-identity. By understanding who you are, what you stand for, and what you desire in life, you can form connections that resonate with your authentic self. In the chapters that follow, we'll build upon this foundation, exploring how to bring your self-identity into your relationships and empower them with honesty, depth, and purpose.

3

Chapter 3: Nurturing Self-Love

I n this chapter, we embark on a profound journey of self-discovery and self-compassion. To build healthy relationships, it's imperative to cultivate a deep and abiding love for oneself. Self-love is not a luxury but a necessity that forms the bedrock of our connections with others.

Defining Self-Love

Self-love is a gentle embrace of all that you are, flaws and all. It's the unconditional acceptance of yourself, the belief that you are worthy of love, care, and respect. In this chapter, we explore what self-love truly means and why it's vital for building healthy relationships.

Overcoming Self-Criticism

Many women grapple with self-criticism and self-doubt. We explore the roots of these negative self-perceptions and provide strategies to challenge and overcome them. As you learn to quiet your inner critic, you'll create space for self-love to flourish.

Self-Care as a Reflection of Self-Love

Self-care is a tangible expression of self-love. We delve into the importance of nurturing your physical, emotional, and mental well-being. From setting boundaries to practicing self-compassion, this chapter guides you in making self-care an integral part of your life.

Healing from Past Wounds

Unresolved past experiences can cast shadows over our self-love. This chapter discusses how to heal from emotional wounds and let go of baggage that may be holding you back. As you free yourself from past burdens, you'll find more room for self-love to thrive.

Embracing Imperfections

Perfection is an elusive ideal that often leads to self-criticism. We encourage you to embrace your imperfections as part of what makes you unique. Self-love thrives in the acceptance of your whole self, including the beautiful messiness that is inherent to being human.

The Ripple Effect of Self-Love

As you nurture self-love, you'll discover that it has a profound impact on your relationships. People are drawn to those who radiate self-confidence, self-acceptance, and self-respect. By loving yourself, you become a magnet for healthy, loving connections.

Practical Exercises and Reflections

Throughout this chapter, you'll find practical exercises and self-reflection prompts designed to help you develop and strengthen self-love. These tools will guide you in your personal journey toward greater self-compassion and self-acceptance.

Nurturing self-love is a transformative journey, one that has the potential to change your relationship with yourself and with others. By learning to love and care for yourself, you'll not only build a stronger foundation for healthy connections but also become a beacon of empowerment and inspiration to those around you.

4

Chapter 4: Embracing Vulnerability

Vulnerability is a gateway to deeper, more authentic connections with others. In this chapter, we explore the power of vulnerability and provide guidance on how to embrace it as a strength rather than a weakness in your relationships.

Defining Vulnerability

Vulnerability is the courage to show your true self, including your fears, insecurities, and emotions. It's about allowing yourself to be seen and heard without pretense. We discuss the significance of embracing vulnerability and dispel myths that might hold you back.

The Fear of Vulnerability

Many women fear vulnerability because it can feel uncomfortable and expose us to the risk of rejection or judgment. We delve into these fears and offer strategies to overcome them. You'll learn how vulnerability can be a path to profound connection and growth.

The Connection Between Vulnerability and Trust

Trust is an essential element of any healthy relationship, and vulnerability is intricately tied to trust. This chapter explores how being vulnerable can help build and strengthen trust in your relationships.

Communication as a Tool for Vulnerability

Effective communication is a key to vulnerability. We provide practical tips for expressing your thoughts and feelings openly and honestly, as well as for actively listening to others. These skills will allow you to connect more deeply with those you care about.

Boundaries and Vulnerability

Embracing vulnerability doesn't mean surrendering your boundaries. We discuss how to set and maintain healthy boundaries while still being open and vulnerable in your relationships. This balance is crucial for ensuring your emotional well-being.

The Rewards of Vulnerability

We explore the rewards of vulnerability, from enhanced emotional intimacy in romantic relationships to deeper connections with friends and family. You'll see how being open and authentic can lead to greater acceptance and understanding from those around you.

Exercises for Practicing Vulnerability

Throughout the chapter, you'll find practical exercises and scenarios to help you practice vulnerability in safe and controlled ways. These exercises will empower you to embrace your authentic self and foster genuine connections with others.

Embracing vulnerability can be both liberating and transformative. As you journey through this chapter and practice being vulnerable, you'll uncover the beauty in your imperfections, deepen your connections, and pave the way for more meaningful and fulfilling relationships in your life.

5

Chapter 5: Effective Communication

Communication is the lifeblood of any relationship. In this chapter, we explore the art of effective communication, which is essential for building and sustaining healthy connections. Whether it's with a partner, family member, friend, or colleague, mastering communication is key to understanding, empathy, and conflict resolution.

The Importance of Effective Communication

Communication is not just about words; it's about the exchange of thoughts, emotions, and ideas. We discuss why effective communication is crucial for building trust, resolving conflicts, and deepening connections in all aspects of life.

Active Listening

Listening is a cornerstone of communication. We delve into the art of active listening, which involves not only hearing the words but also understanding the emotions and intentions behind them. You'll learn how to be fully present in conversations and show others that you genuinely care.

Expressing Your Thoughts and Feelings

We provide practical advice on how to express yourself with clarity and authenticity. This includes techniques for sharing your thoughts, emotions, and needs honestly and openly while avoiding common pitfalls that can lead to misunderstandings.

Nonverbal Communication

Communication isn't limited to words; nonverbal cues play a significant role. We explore the impact of body language, facial expressions, and tone of voice in conveying emotions and intentions. Understanding nonverbal communication can enhance your ability to connect with others.

Conflict Resolution Through Communication

Conflict is a natural part of relationships, but it can also be an opportunity for growth and understanding. We provide strategies for resolving conflicts in a healthy and constructive manner. Learning to communicate effectively during conflicts is a valuable skill for maintaining strong connections.

Digital Communication

In our digital age, many relationships involve online and text-based communication. We discuss the challenges and opportunities of digital communication and offer tips on how to maintain meaningful connections in the digital realm.

Cultivating Empathy

Empathy is the ability to understand and share the feelings of another. We explore the role of empathy in communication and how it can lead to deeper and more meaningful connections. You'll learn techniques for enhancing your empathy and connecting on a more profound level with others.

Exercises for Improving Communication

Throughout the chapter, you'll find practical exercises and scenarios designed to enhance your communication skills. These exercises will empower you to become a more effective communicator, fostering understanding and intimacy in your relationships.

Mastering effective communication is an ongoing process, but the rewards are immense. As you immerse yourself in this chapter, you'll develop the skills to express yourself authentically, connect with others on a deeper level, and navigate the challenges of communication with confidence and grace.

6

Chapter 6: Building Trust and Trusting Intuition

Trust is the cornerstone of healthy and fulfilling relationships. In this chapter, we delve into the complex and often delicate art of building trust with others and, equally important, learning to trust your own intuition.

Understanding Trust

Trust is the foundation upon which all meaningful relationships are built. We explore the components of trust, including reliability, honesty, and vulnerability. Trust is the bridge that allows people to connect deeply, knowing they can rely on each other.

The Role of Self-Trust

Before we can trust others, we must trust ourselves. We discuss self-trust and the importance of listening to your intuition. Learning to trust your own judgment and instincts is a vital part of fostering healthy relationships.

Building Trust in Relationships

We provide strategies for building and maintaining trust in various types of relationships, from romantic partnerships to friendships and professional connections. You'll learn how open and honest communication, consistency, and reliability are key factors in trust-building.

Recognizing and Healing Trust Issues

Many of us carry trust issues from past experiences. We discuss how to recognize and heal these issues, allowing you to move forward with more open and trusting relationships. Understanding the roots of your trust issues can be a profound step toward personal growth.

The Importance of Boundaries

Boundaries play a significant role in trust. We explore how setting and respecting boundaries in your relationships can foster trust and respect. Establishing clear boundaries is a way of communicating your needs and limits, ensuring both parties feel safe and understood.

Trusting Your Intuition

Intuition is a powerful guiding force in our lives. We discuss the significance of listening to your intuition and provide tips on how to differentiate between intuition and fear. Trusting your inner wisdom is key to making sound decisions in relationships.

Rebuilding Trust After Betrayal

When trust is broken, it can be challenging to rebuild. We offer guidance on how to navigate the process of rebuilding trust after a breach. Rebuilding trust requires patience, understanding, and open communication.

Exercises for Building Trust

Throughout the chapter, you'll find exercises and reflection prompts to help you explore trust in your relationships and practice trusting your intuition. These tools will empower you to strengthen the trust within yourself and with others.

Building trust and trusting your intuition are ongoing processes. This chapter will equip you with the knowledge and tools to nurture trust in your relationships and to follow your intuition with confidence, ultimately leading to deeper and more fulfilling connections with others.

7

Chapter 7: Friendship and Support Networks

Friendships are a vital aspect of a woman's life, providing support, companionship, and a sense of belonging. In this chapter, we explore the significance of friendship and how to cultivate a robust support network.

The Importance of Friendships

Friendships are often the unsung heroes of our lives, providing emotional support, laughter, and shared experiences. We delve into why friendships are essential for overall well-being and how they contribute to our personal growth.

Types of Friendships

Not all friendships are created equal. We discuss the different types of friendships, from close confidants to more casual acquaintances, and how each type serves a unique role in our lives. Understanding the dynamics of these friendships can help you manage and nurture them effectively.

Support Networks

Building a support network is essential for navigating life's challenges. We explore the concept of support networks, which encompass friends, family, mentors, and others who provide emotional, practical, and psychological support. We'll guide you in creating and maintaining a reliable network.

The Dynamics of Female Friendships

Female friendships often come with their own dynamics and complexities. We discuss the unique aspects of women's friendships, including emotional depth, communication, and the role of mutual support. Understanding these dynamics can help you build stronger female friendships.

Toxic Friendships and Setting Boundaries

Not all friendships are healthy. We address the issue of toxic friendships and provide guidance on recognizing and addressing them. We also explore the importance of setting boundaries in all friendships to maintain your emotional well-being.

Nurturing Friendships

Friendships require effort and nurturing. We offer tips on how to maintain and strengthen your friendships, including active listening, being present, and making an effort to stay connected, even in busy lives.

Building New Friendships

Life often brings us new opportunities to build friendships. We discuss strategies for making new friends, whether you're in a new city, entering a different life stage, or simply looking to expand your social circle.

Exercises for Cultivating Friendships

Throughout the chapter, you'll find exercises and reflection prompts to help you assess and nurture your friendships. These tools will empower you to build and maintain strong, supportive friendships that enhance your life.

Friendships and support networks are an essential part of a woman's life. As you delve into this chapter, you'll gain insights into the dynamics of friendships and learn how to build and maintain meaningful connections with the women who lift you up and provide companionship on your life journey.

8

Chapter 8: Romantic Relationships

Romantic relationships hold a special place in many women's lives. They are a source of love, passion, and personal growth. In this chapter, we explore the intricacies of romantic relationships, including their dynamics, challenges, and keys to building lasting love.

Defining Healthy Romantic Relationships

What constitutes a healthy romantic relationship? We begin by defining the qualities that make a romantic relationship fulfilling, supportive, and nourishing. Understanding these characteristics is crucial for creating a strong foundation.

Understanding Love Languages

Each of us expresses and receives love differently. We explore the concept of love languages and how understanding your partner's and your own love language can transform your relationship. Learning to speak each other's love languages is a key to fostering intimacy.

Embracing Emotional Intimacy

Emotional intimacy is a cornerstone of a strong romantic relationship. We delve into the importance of opening up, being vulnerable, and creating a safe space for emotional connection. Strategies for enhancing emotional intimacy are shared.

Maintaining Healthy Boundaries

Boundaries in romantic relationships are essential to ensure both partners feel respected and secure. We discuss the importance of setting and respecting boundaries and offer guidance on navigating the delicate balance between individuality and togetherness.

Effective Conflict Resolution

Conflict is a natural part of any relationship. We provide strategies for handling conflicts in a constructive manner, fostering understanding, and maintaining a healthy connection. Conflict resolution skills are a crucial component of lasting love.

Navigating Life Transitions

Life is a journey of change, and relationships evolve with it. We discuss how to navigate life transitions, from career changes to family planning, and how to ensure your relationship thrives through these transformations.

Long-Term Commitment and Sustainability

Many women aspire to long-term, committed relationships. We explore the keys to maintaining a sustainable, loving partnership over the years. Topics include communication, adaptation, and keeping the romance alive.

Exercises for Strengthening Romantic Relationships

Throughout the chapter, you'll find exercises and reflection prompts to help you assess and strengthen your romantic relationship. These tools will empower you to build and maintain a loving and lasting connection with your partner.

Romantic relationships have the power to be a source of great joy and fulfillment. As you delve into this chapter, you'll gain insights into the dynamics of romantic relationships and learn how to create and sustain a deep and meaningful connection with your partner, fostering a love that lasts.

9

Chapter 9: Family Dynamics and Connection

Family is often the cornerstone of our lives, providing support, love, and a sense of belonging. In this chapter, we delve into the complexities of family dynamics and explore how to maintain healthy connections within your family.

The Importance of Family Connection

Family is where we first learn about relationships, values, and love. We begin by discussing the significance of family connections and how they impact our well-being and personal growth.

Understanding Family Dynamics

Families have their unique dynamics, from sibling rivalries to generational differences. We explore the intricacies of family relationships and offer insights into understanding and navigating these dynamics effectively.

Healing Family Wounds

Many of us carry unresolved wounds from our family past. We discuss the process of healing family wounds, whether it's dealing with conflicts, misunderstandings, or unmet expectations. Healing these wounds can lead to healthier and more fulfilling family connections.

Fostering Connection Within Your Family

We provide strategies for fostering stronger family connections, including open communication, spending quality time together, and creating shared traditions. Strengthening the bonds within your family can lead to a more supportive and loving environment.

Balancing Autonomy and Family Ties

As we grow and change, striking a balance between autonomy and maintaining close family relationships can be challenging. We explore the importance of setting boundaries and maintaining your independence while still fostering strong family connections.

Supporting Family Members Through Challenges

Families go through tough times. We discuss strategies for supporting family members during challenging moments, from illness and loss to life transitions. Being there for your family can deepen the bonds and provide comfort during times of need.

Exercises for Nurturing Family Connections

Throughout the chapter, you'll find exercises and reflection prompts to help you assess and nurture your family connections. These tools will empower you to create and maintain strong, supportive, and loving bonds within your family.

Family dynamics and connections are central to a woman's life. As you explore this chapter, you'll gain insights into the complexities of family relationships and learn how to foster stronger, more resilient connections with your loved ones, creating a supportive network that nurtures your growth and well-being.

10

Chapter 10: Balancing Independence and Interdependence

Balancing the need for independence with the desire for interdependence is an intricate dance in personal and relational growth. In this chapter, we explore the art of maintaining your individuality while participating in interconnected, meaningful relationships.

The Dance of Independence and Interdependence

We begin by discussing the concepts of independence and interdependence and how they manifest in different aspects of life. This chapter aims to help you understand the balance between self-reliance and shared experiences.

The Importance of Independence

Independence is the foundation of personal growth and self-discovery. We explore why it's essential to maintain your independence even within close relationships. Being self-reliant empowers you to bring your whole self to your connections.

Nurturing Independence Within Relationships

We offer strategies for nurturing your independence within various relationships, including romantic partnerships, family, and friendships. Maintaining your individuality can enhance the quality and depth of your connections.

Embracing Interdependence

Interdependence is the art of balancing autonomy and connection. We discuss the significance of interdependence and how it strengthens relationships by creating a sense of shared purpose and mutual support.

Setting Boundaries to Maintain Independence

Effective boundaries are essential for preserving independence. We delve into the role of boundaries in relationships and provide guidance on how to set and maintain them to ensure you stay true to yourself.

Communication as the Key to Balance

Effective communication is the bridge between independence and interdependence. We explore how open and honest communication can help you navigate the balance between autonomy and connection in your relationships.

Exercises for Balancing Independence and Interdependence

Throughout the chapter, you'll find exercises and reflection prompts to help you assess and nurture your independence within relationships. These tools will empower you to find equilibrium between your individuality and your interconnectedness, creating relationships that enhance your personal growth.

Balancing independence and interdependence is a skill that evolves over time.

As you immerse yourself in this chapter, you'll gain insights into maintaining your autonomy while fostering deeper, more meaningful connections with others. This balance will empower you to enjoy the best of both worlds— personal growth and fulfilling relationships.

11

Chapter 11: Conflict Resolution and Boundaries

onflict is a natural part of any relationship, but how we address and resolve conflicts can make or break the connection. In this chapter, we explore the importance of effective conflict resolution and the role of boundaries in maintaining healthy relationships.

Understanding Conflict

We begin by defining what conflict is and why it's a regular occurrence in relationships. It's essential to accept that conflicts will arise and that they can be opportunities for growth and understanding.

The Impact of Unresolved Conflict

Unresolved conflicts can lead to resentment and emotional distance. We discuss how failing to address conflicts can harm relationships and hinder personal growth. Understanding the consequences of unresolved issues is the first step toward healthier conflict resolution.

Setting Healthy Boundaries

Boundaries are the framework that guides how we interact with others. We explore the significance of setting and maintaining healthy boundaries in relationships. Understanding and respecting each other's boundaries is crucial for conflict prevention and resolution.

Communication During Conflict

Effective communication during conflict is the key to resolution. We provide strategies for expressing your thoughts, emotions, and needs openly and honestly, as well as for actively listening to the other party. Learning to communicate effectively during conflicts fosters understanding and connection.

Conflict Resolution Styles

We delve into different conflict resolution styles, from avoiding conflict to accommodating, compromising, collaborating, and competing. Understanding your own style and your partner's style can help you navigate conflicts more effectively.

The Art of Compromise

Compromise is often the path to resolution. We explore how to find common ground, negotiate, and make concessions without sacrificing your own needs and boundaries. Compromise is a valuable skill for maintaining strong connections.

Forgiveness and Healing

Forgiveness is an essential part of conflict resolution. We discuss the power of forgiveness in healing emotional wounds and moving forward. Learning to forgive allows you to release negative emotions and rebuild trust.

Exercises for Effective Conflict Resolution and Boundary Setting

Throughout the chapter, you'll find exercises and reflection prompts to help you practice effective conflict resolution and boundary setting in your relationships. These tools will empower you to navigate conflicts with grace and strength, ultimately leading to deeper, more resilient connections with others.

Conflict resolution and boundary setting are vital skills in maintaining healthy relationships. As you dive into this chapter, you'll gain insights into the dynamics of conflict and learn how to resolve issues with respect, empathy, and open communication. These skills will empower you to strengthen your connections and create relationships that are built on understanding and mutual respect.

12

Chapter 12: Sustaining Healthy Relationships Over Time

Sustaining healthy relationships is a lifelong endeavor, and in this final chapter, we explore the strategies and principles for maintaining strong and fulfilling connections with others over time.

The Journey of Relationship Growth

Relationships are dynamic, ever-evolving entities. We begin by discussing the concept of relationship growth, which involves navigating the various stages of connections, from initial attraction to deep, enduring bonds.

Consistent Communication

Effective communication is the lifeblood of a long-lasting relationship. We emphasize the importance of maintaining open, honest, and consistent communication as you navigate the ups and downs of life together.

Cultivating Emotional Intimacy

Emotional intimacy is the heart of enduring relationships. We explore the ways in which you can continue to foster emotional connection with your loved ones, even after years of togetherness.

Adapting to Life Changes

Life is filled with changes, both expected and unexpected. We discuss strategies for adapting to life changes, such as career shifts, relocation, and family dynamics. Adapting together is key to sustaining a strong connection.

Celebrating Milestones and Shared Moments

Celebrating milestones and creating shared memories is vital for relationship longevity. We explore the power of rituals, traditions, and celebrating special moments as ways to keep the flame of connection alive.

Self-Care in Relationships

Self-care isn't just an individual practice; it's crucial for sustaining healthy relationships. We discuss the importance of self-care and the role it plays in maintaining your well-being, which, in turn, benefits your relationships.

Respecting Autonomy and Independence

Respecting each other's autonomy and independence is an ongoing endeavor. We emphasize the significance of maintaining personal space and boundaries while still nurturing your interconnectedness.

Expressing Appreciation and Gratitude

Appreciation and gratitude are essential elements of long-lasting relationships. We discuss the power of expressing love and gratitude for your loved ones, and how this can enhance the quality of your connections.

Exercises for Sustaining Healthy Relationships

Throughout the chapter, you'll find exercises and reflection prompts to help you continue to strengthen your connections and keep your relationships vibrant and resilient. These tools will empower you to navigate the challenges and joys of long-term relationships with grace and purpose.

Sustaining healthy relationships over time is a rewarding journey. As you conclude this book, you'll be equipped with insights and skills to maintain deep, meaningful connections with your loved ones, ensuring that your relationships continue to enrich your life and provide support and love for years to come.

www.ingramcontent.com/pod-product-compliance
Lightning Source LLC
LaVergne TN
LVHW051245200726
843510LV00011B/1690